Blasts from the Past

Look for other

titles:

World's Weirdest Critters
Creepy Stuff
Odd-inary People
Amazing Escapes
Bizarre Bugs
World's Weirdest Gadgets

Blasts
from the
Past

by Mary Packard

and the Editors of Ripley Entertainment Inc.

illustrations by Leanne Franson

SCHOLASTIC INC.

New York   Toronto   London   Auckland   Sydney
Mexico City   New Delhi   Hong Kong   Buenos Aires

Developed by Nancy Hall, Inc.
Designed by R studio T
Cover design by Atif Toor
Photo research by Laura Miller

ISBN 0-439-42980-3

12 11 10 9 8 7 6 5 4 3 2 1   3 4 5 6 7 8/0

Printed in the U.S.A.
First printing, March 2003

Contents

Blasts
from the
Past

Introduction

Ripley Takes on the Past

The past is filled with little-known facts that you probably won't find in your history books. These are the kind of facts that fascinated Robert Ripley, creator of Believe It or Not! The first cartoonist to become a millionaire, Ripley liked to illustrate historical facts that would surprise, shock, or amuse his readers. To Ripley,  the fact that George Washington had lost all but one tooth by his mid-fifties and had six sets of dentures was far more interesting than conventional facts such as where or when Washington was born.

Perhaps Ripley's fascination with the most remarkable aspects of history is one reason why he made sure that the hours and days of his own life were so memorable.

An avid traveler, Ripley visited 201 countries during his lifetime. He loved to explore out-of-the-way places, making grueling treks into remote regions, often on the back of a donkey or a camel.

One place Ripley could not get enough of was China. Charmed by its sheer antiquity, he returned again and

again. The tombs of the Ming Dynasty (1368–1644) filled Ripley with awe, as did the larger-than-life-sized carved stone animals and warriors surrounding them. Because elephants are not native to China, the stone elephants are evidence of contact between China and Thailand at the time the tombs were built. This was the way that Ripley liked to learn about history—with three-dimensional clues that brought the past to life for him.

The Ripley archives are filled with quirky stories from the past featuring famous characters whose behavior was more than a little offbeat—people like King George II, who was saved from enemy soldiers by a loyalist who hid him beneath her hoop skirt, or the Earl of Derby, whose dying wish was that two roosters be brought to his sickroom so that he could watch them fight.

Ripley assured his own place in history when he declared in a 1929 cartoon: "America Has No National Anthem." After the cartoon appeared, enormous public demand led to Congress declaring "The Star-Spangled Banner" the official national anthem just over a year later.

Think history's a bore? *Blasts from the Past* is filled with stories like these that just might change your mind. See how much you already know about the past by taking the One for the Books! quizzes and the Ripley's Brain Buster in each chapter. Then try your hand at the Pop Quiz at the end of the book and figure out your Ripley's rank with the handy scorecard.

Remember—Robert Ripley made history. Maybe you can, too!

Believe It!®

CHAPTER 1

Can You Dig It?

The mysteries of the past are solved by detectives called archaeologists, who use shovels, picks, chisels, and *lots* of brainpower.

One for the Books!

Picture-writing dating back to the caveman era was found above the entrance to a cave. Roughly translated, the message said which of the following?

a. Welcome!
b. Please wipe your feet.
c. Keep out!
d. Beware of bats.

Old As Dirt: In 1952, 13-year-old Donald Baldwin discovered a 5,000-year-old burial ground in Oconto, Wisconsin. It belonged to the Copper Culture people, who were one of the first in the world to make forged copper tools such as the awls, spear points, and fish hooks that were found at the site.

Long Live the King:

In ancient times, civilization thrived in Mesopotamia, a fertile area between the Tigris and Euphrates rivers that is now part of Iraq. Every New Year— or whenever the omens were very bad—the people of Mesopotamia sacrificed the life of their king to please the gods. Actually, the real king

took the day off and some other poor soul was chosen to be king for the day. In 1861 B.C.E., Enlil-Bani was the king's stand-in. Just as the noose was about to be placed around his neck, an unbelievable thing happened. A messenger rushed in with news that the real king had just died. Enlil-Bani was spared and went on to rule the kingdom for 24 years.

Hard to Swallow:

Archaeologists in Sweden discovered the world's oldest chewing gum—a 9,000-year-old piece of birch resin with teeth marks in it.

One for the Books!

When the grave of a Neanderthal man buried 60,000 years ago was opened, it was found to contain . . .

a. a pet monkey.
b. flowers.
c. a necklace made from a mammoth tusk.
d. a portrait of a loved one.

Tall Story: Mysterious burial mounds found across the United States must have been built by a prehistoric race of giants. All the skeletons of adults found beneath the mounds were seven to eight feet long.

Hole in the Head: Evidence of trepanning, the oldest form of brain surgery, has been found in skulls dating as far back as 40,000 years ago.

Sharp-Tongued:

Robert Ripley traveled to Mexico City, where he posed with the Aztec Calendar Stone. Unearthed in 1760, the stone is nearly 12 feet wide and weighs more than 20 tons. Its carvings record what the Aztecs believed were the first four epochs of the world and show the 18 months of the Aztec year. The calendar reveals that the Aztecs had a knowledge of astronomy, but it is also evidence of something more primitive. At the stone's center, the Aztec sun god sticks out its knife-shaped tongue, a grim reminder of the food it required from its worshipers—human blood and hearts.

One for the Books!

The Aztecs were the first to . . .

a. put candles on birthday cakes.
b. create cartoons with speech balloons.
c. play table tennis.
d. make rock candy.

Busybody: Over the course of his lifetime, Pliny the Elder (23–79 C.E.) was governor of Germany, Gaul, Spain, and Africa, as well as both a general and an admiral in the armed forces of ancient Rome. During this time, he wrote a 37-volume encyclopedia of natural history, a 31-volume history of Rome, a 20-volume history of Roman warfare, a six-volume manual of public speaking, and eight books

of Latin grammar. When Mount Vesuvius erupted, Pliny sailed toward Herculanium instead of away from it, taking notes all the while. His notes survived the disaster, but, sadly, Pliny did not.

Same Old, Same Old:

Archaeologists excavating Roman ruins along Hadrian's wall in northern England have unearthed clothing, shoes, letters, tax records—even a 2,000-year-old invitation to a birthday celebration that includes the first known sample of a woman's handwriting in Latin.

Breaking the News: In ancient times, scribes were often the only people who could read and write. Fearing that scribes would write bad things about them, the rulers of invading armies made sure to round them up before anyone else. In ancient Maya, for example, conquering rulers ensured that their prisoners' writing days were over by having their fingers broken and their fingernails torn out!

Taking Notes: It's been known for a while that the ancient Sumerians of Mesopotamia kept written records on clay tablets as long ago as 3300 B.C.E. But scientists have recently discovered that they kept track of merchandise on small clay *tokens* as much as 5,000 years earlier!

One for the Books!

An amazing find provided a clue that life can exist even inside a 4,000-year-old Egyptian mummy case. What was it?

a. Dormant dragonfly larvae.
b. A seed from which flowers were subsequently grown.
c. New hair growth on the mummy.
d. Cockroach eggs that hatched after the coffin was opened.

Picture This: In ancient Egypt, a system of picture-writing called hieroglyphics was used until about 400 C.E. So how is it that scholars are able to translate a form of writing that died out over 1,600 years ago? A stone tablet called the Rosetta Stone is the answer. Discovered in Egypt in 1799, the stone has three different scripts carved into it: Greek, Egyptian hieroglyphics, and demotic, a late form of Egyptian writing.

The easily translated Greek served as a key for deciphering the hieroglyphics. What does the writing say? Lots of good things about the ruling pharaoh, of course. Seems the scribe who wrote it was playing it safe!

Holy Smoke: To enter certain ancient Greek and Egyptian temples, you had to know the secret. Mysterious hidden doors would open only when a fire was lit on a special altar outside.

Breaking the Rules: When her husband, the pharaoh, died, Hatshepsut was supposed to rule until her son was old enough to take the throne. But she liked her job so much that she declared herself pharaoh and appeared before her subjects wearing a phony beard—because beards

were a symbol of power. Hatshepsut's reign extended from 1503 to 1482 B.C.E., breaking the 2,000-year-tradition of male-only rule. Unlike the pharaohs before her, she was devoted to peace and prosperity and opposed to waging war.

Under Wraps: To make a mummy, Egyptian embalmers used 400 pounds of natron salt (sodium carbonate) and 150 yards of linen strips.

Mummy's Day:

In 1996, a temple guard in Egypt discovered the largest number of mummies ever found in one place—and he wasn't even looking for them! The donkey he was riding got its hoof stuck in what the guard thought was a small pothole. As he gently removed the donkey's hoof, he peered through the hole

and saw many amazingly well-preserved mummies covered with gold. Archaeologists estimate that there are 10,000 bodies in the two square miles of what is now known as the Valley of the Golden Mummies. Though some of them wear gold masks, others wear carved masks painted with lifelike portraits. One mummy sports rows of carved red curls beneath her crown.

One for the Books!

To cure a sick baby, mothers in ancient Egypt would sometimes eat a . . .

a. scarab beetle.
b. camel's eye.
c. mouse.
d. raw ostrich egg.

Anybody Home?

Archaeologists digging under the leaning tower of Pisa in 1992 discovered an ancient Roman house. Complete with furniture and dinner plates, the house was less than three feet below ground level.

A Mammoth Job: Taller at the shoulder than a double-decker bus, the mammoth was one of the largest land mammals that ever lived. Neanderthal men and women ate its meat, wore its skin, and used its oily bones to keep their fires burning and its tusks to fasten roofs to their dwellings. How did hunters slay these huge beasts? With nothing more than rocks and flint-tipped wooden spears!

Lighting the Way: An ingenious lighting system was discovered in a series of caves in Hal Saflieni Hypogeum on the island of Malta. Constructed 5,000 years ago, the highly polished stone walls enabled a single ray of sunlight to illuminate the entire labyrinth.

Rolling Stones: The first taxicab in history was unearthed by archaeologists in Rome. The 2,000-year-old horse-drawn carriage was equipped with a meter that dropped pebbles into a drum when a rear wheel revolved. Counting the pebbles determined the amount of the fare.

One for the Books!

To ensure the privacy of ancient stone writings, the very first envelopes were made out of . . .

a. mammoth skin.
b. mud.
c. dung.
d. wax.

Ceiled Fate: Anastasius I (c. 430–518 C.E.), emperor of Byzantium, was warned that he would be killed by lightning. No doubt that is why he always ran for shelter at the slightest hint of a storm. One stormy day, Anastasius ran into an old house to avoid the lightning. Big mistake! The ceiling came crashing down and crushed him to death.

Boar Lore: According to legend, Diocletian (c. 245–313 C.E.) was told by a prophet that he would become emperor of Rome by killing a wild boar. After he learned to hunt, he killed lots of wild boars. But it was not until he stabbed the assassin of Emperor Numerian to death that

Diocletian was crowned emperor of Rome. What did the assassin's name mean in Latin? Wild Boar.

Faces of the Past: Easter Island, about 2,000 miles west of South America, is known throughout the world for the gigantic statues called Moai that dot the island. Created about 700 years ago by a lost culture, these eerie disembodied heads (*see cover*) stand an average of 20 feet tall and weigh about 18 tons. Stone tools were used to carve the statues from the rock in the crater of an extinct volcano. Then the islanders moved the statues up to 14 miles away to stone platforms, called *ahu*—even though the islanders had no horses or oxen to pull them. How? No one really knows.

One for the Books!

If the age of Earth were represented by a 12-hour clock, the entire written history of humanity would represent . . .

a. four hours.
b. fifteen minutes.
c. one hour.
d. eight seconds.

Brain Buster

Sometimes truth really is stranger than fiction. And now it's your turn to tell the difference in these out-of-the-ordinary activities!

Robert Ripley dedicated his life to seeking out the bizarre and unusual. But every unbelievable thing he recorded was known to be true. In the Brain Busters at the end of every chapter, you'll play Ripley's role—trying to verify the fantastic facts presented. Each Ripley's Brain Buster contains a group of four shocking statements. But of these so-called "facts," **one** is **fiction**. Will you **Believe It!** or **Not!**?

Wait—there's more! Following the Brain Busters are special bonus games in which you'll try to solve a tricky "History Mystery." To see how you rate, flip to the end of the book for answer keys and a scorecard.

Ancient arti-fact or fiction? Of the following four fantastic facts, one is pure fantasy. Can you unearth the one imposter?

a. Danish astronomer Tycho Brahe spent much of his life with a fake nose made of gold and silver.

Believe It!   **Not!**

b. In 1984, archaeologist Rachel Jordan excavated what scientists believe is a prehistoric baseball field. Jordan's work suggests that a primitive type of the game may have been played by Neanderthals.

Believe It!   **Not!**

c. An old wooden bridge spanned Kangaroo Valley in New South Wales, Australia, for nearly 100 years. On February 8, 1898, it was replaced by a modern suspension bridge. Six days later, the old bridge was destroyed by a flood.

Believe It!   **Not!**

d. A finger of ancient astronomer Galileo Galilei is on display at the Institute and Museum of the History of Science in Florence, Italy.

Believe It!   **Not!**

• •

BONUS GAME—HISTORY MYSTERY

A certain transformation in 1918 shifted the way that Americans considered their days and time in general. One day, it was declared that the sun would set later. And people had to get out of bed earlier! This sudden change is still in effect today. What happened in the United States in 1918 to change people's days so drastically?

CHAPTER 2 The Good Old Days?

Maybe, but on closer inspection, it seems some days were good, some were weird, and others were downright disgusting!

Digest This! During the Middle Ages, 20 years of chopping off people's heads qualified executioners to become doctors. But in order to practice medicine, a physician had to know Latin. Since most executioners were not bilingual, some of them swallowed the pages of Latin dictionaries in the hopes that it would help them become fluent in the language!

One for the Books!
Catherine the Great of Russia suffered a fatal stroke while . . .

a. brushing her teeth.
b. sitting on the commode.
c. watching an opera.
d. riding her horse.

To Be or Bea or Not to Bee:

In Elizabethan England, no one worried about spelling. That's because the idea of always spelling something the same way was still very new. As a matter of fact, not even William Shakespeare (1564–1616) was consistent. The famous playwright signed his name several different ways at different times. Shagspeare, Shakespeare, and Shaxpere are just a few of them.

Pop Goes the Casket:

While on display in London, the casket of Queen Elizabeth I (1533–1603) mysteriously exploded on the night before she was to be buried. The coffin was destroyed, yet the queen's body was unharmed.

One for the Books!

Public urinals were a source of income for Emperor Vespasian (C.E. 9–79) of Rome, who had the urine collected so the ammonia could be used . . .

a. as ant killer.
b. to clean windows.
c. in fabric dyes.
d. to unclog drains.

No Joke: In 1634, Nicolas François and his wife, Claude, the Duke and Duchess of Lorraine, in France, were sentenced to death and imprisoned in the ducal palace of Nancy. On April 1, they climbed out a window and swam across the river Meurthe to safety.

Witnesses shouted an alarm, but the guards did nothing because they thought it was just an April Fool's joke.

Royal Flush: Maria Letizia Ramolino (1750–1836) is known as the "mother of monarchs." Her children were: Napoléon, who became emperor of France; Joseph, who became king of Spain; Jérôme, who became king of Westphalia; Louis, who became king of Holland; Caroline, who became queen of Naples; Lucien, who became prince of Canino; Élisa, who became grand duchess of Tuscany; and Pauline, who became duchess of Guastalla.

Lousy Choice:
In 19th-century Sweden, a new burgomaster, or mayor, was chosen by placing a louse in the center of a table. The man whose beard the insect jumped into held the office for the next year.

One for the Books!

Emperor Akbar (1542–1605) of India forced every candidate for high office to compete with him in a game of . . .

a. night polo—using balls of fire.
b. chess—while wearing blindfolds.
c. water polo—in a pool filled with sharks.
d. croquet—using balls filled with gunpowder.

Handy Victory:
In 1015 B.C.E., Heremon O'Neill had a boating race with a rival chieftain. The first man to touch Ireland's soil would win the land. O'Neill won by cutting off his own hand and hurling it ashore, a sacrifice that made him the first king of Ulster.

By the Book:

Commentaries on the Laws of England, written by Sir William Blackstone (1723–1780), became the most influential book in the history of English law. During a session of parliament, Blackstone was proven wrong on a legal point by his own book!

Not in the Pink:

Emperor Chi'en-lung (1711–1799), considered by many to be China's wisest ruler, was switched at birth. His mother substituted the son of a court servant for her own baby girl because she was afraid to tell the emperor his child was not a boy.

Mother of Pearls: Some people believe that Mother Goose was a real person. Even though the term originated in France, one American woman is often credited with the name. Elizabeth Foster (1665–c.1756)

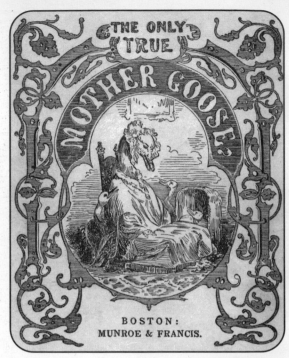

THE ONLY TRUE MOTHER GOOSE

BOSTON:
MUNROE & FRANCIS.

married Isaac Goose in 1692 and later told her grandchildren the famous rhymes—most of which came from England. The story goes that Goose's son-in-law published the rhymes in 1719, but there are no copies of the book and no proof that it was ever printed.

One for the Books!

Humpty Dumpty is really about a . . .

a. scrambled egg.
b. king who lost a war.
c. prince who fell into a moat.
d. thief who fell off a wall.

Baa, Baa Black Sheep:

Have you any wool? Yes, sir, yes, sir, three bags full. One for my master, and one for my dame. And one for the little boy who lives down the lane. Many people think this nursery rhyme was written as a complaint about taxes. The "master" was the king while "dame" stood for the rich nobility. The "little boy" was the peasant who did all the work but got just a third of the profits of his labor.

Little Jack Horner . . . *sat in a corner eating his Christmas pie. He stuck in a thumb, pulled out a plum, and said, "What a good boy am I."* To discourage robbers, deeds to King Henry VIII's properties were baked into a pie. Jack Horner was the messenger who was to deliver the deeds to the king. Legend has it that Horner wasn't so good after all, because he couldn't resist reaching into the pie and taking one of the king's deeds for himself. Seems everyone heard about the heist but King Henry!

Scents and Sensibility: In the country, people used outhouses, called privies, to relieve themselves. Privies were foul-smelling and attracted flies. Perhaps that's why so many rose, lilac, and honeysuckle bushes were planted around them. People hoped the fragrance of the flowers would disguise the pungent odors! The expression "to pluck a rose" was a polite way of saying you were about to go to the privy.

Smelly Old Days: As late as the early 20th century, cities smelled awful. With no running water for flush toilets, poor people in the slums threw their bodily wastes and other types of garbage into the streets. It didn't take much more than a gentle breeze to carry the smells to other parts of the city.

One for the Books!

While emperor of Rome, Caligula (C.E. 12–41) made taking a bath a crime punishable by . . .

a. death.
b. imprisonment.
c. public humiliation.
d. a hefty fine.

Down and Dirty: Not only did the air smell bad in Europe during the 18th century, a lot of the people did, too. Without modern plumbing, many people didn't bathe very often. Some were so confused about hygiene that they thought bathing would cause them to catch a chill and make them sick! Instead, they covered their body odor with heavy perfumes. Pew!

Going to Pot: Victorians may have been shy about their bodies, but no one could say they lacked a sense of humor. Many Victorians used vessels called chamber pots as toilets. Some of them played tunes, others had portraits of politicians painted in the center, and still

others were painted with a large eye. Beneath the eye were the words "Use me well and keep me clean, and I'll not tell what I have seen."

Royal Stink: Not even the royals could avoid the smelly vapors that hung in the air. Once while cruising on the Thames River in England on the royal yacht, Queen Victoria fainted from the stench. Another time a section of Windsor Castle had to be closed because 53 cesspools overflowed at once.

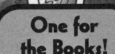

One for the Books!

Queen Isabella of Spain (1451–1504) was proud of the fact that she . . .

a. used fragrant soaps imported from China.
b. had a solid-gold bathtub.
c. had indoor plumbing.
d. had taken only two baths in her life.

 **Brain Buster**

Sometimes the past is better off forgotten. And one of these four facts is *really* worth forgetting—because it isn't even true!

a. The shortest war on record was between Britain and Zanzibar. It lasted 38 minutes.
Believe It!   Not!

b. In the 17th century, people in England had strange cleaning methods. They used ashes, bread, and urine to clean their clothes!
Believe It!   Not!

c. Seventeenth-century French painter Nic Beaumont is believed to have begun the tradition of graffiti. While other artists painted lively Parisian street scenes, Beaumont was busy painting sweeping landscapes *on* the streets.
Believe It!   Not!

d. The state of Tennessee was once known as "Franklin."
Believe It!   Not!

BONUS GAME—HISTORY MYSTERY

When the United States made the Louisiana Purchase, did the government know what a good deal it got? It purchased the land from the Mississippi River to the Rocky Mountains from the French for the bargain price of $15 million. But more amazing is what this amounted to per acre. About how much do you think the United States paid for each acre of land? (Hint: It's less than $1 per acre.)

CHAPTER 3

Back in the U.S.A.

Try finding these little-known presidential facts in your history books!

Who's on First? John Hanson (1721–1783) was the first president of the United States. In 1781, Maryland signed the Articles of Confederation, and the original 13 colonies were officially united. Hanson was elected president by the assembled congress—which included George Washington (1732–1799). In fact, six more presidents were elected before Washington became the first president to serve under the Constitution, which became law in 1788.

One for the Books!

Eight U.S. presidents were born in log cabins. They were Zachary Taylor, James Polk, Franklin Pierce, Abraham Lincoln, Andrew Jackson, Millard Fillmore, James Buchanan, and . . .

a. James Garfield.
b. Teddy Roosevelt.
c. William Taft.
d. John Quincy Adams.

Taking a Stand:

President John Adams (1735–1826) was a lawyer as well as a politician. In 1770, he was asked to defend the British soldiers accused of killing five people in the Boston Massacre. Adams was a patriot, but he decided to defend the enemy soldiers, who he felt had fired in self-defense at the threatening mob of Americans. The jury must have agreed because they acquitted seven of the soldiers and convicted two of manslaughter instead of murder. But feelings ran high in Boston and, because of his actions, Adams lost friends as well as clients.

Handy Trick:

President James Garfield (1831–1881) could write with both hands at once— using one hand to write in Latin and the other to write in Greek!

Justice for All:

President Ulysses S. Grant (1822–1885) loved to race through the streets of Washington, D.C. One day he was stopped for speeding by a police officer, who arrested him. When the officer

realized he had stopped the president, he wanted to let him go. But Grant refused to accept privileged treatment and took his punishment—a fine of $20.

One for the Books!

Abraham Lincoln (1809–1865) was the only president to receive a patent for an invention: a hydraulic system for . . .

a. removing coal from mine shafts.
b. lifting ships over shallow water.
c. raising and lowering swivel chairs.
d. elevators.

Book Smart:

Harry S. Truman (1884–1972) did not attend college, but he was highly educated. By the age of 14 he had read every book in the Independence, Missouri, library. He practiced the piano for two hours every day before he went to school, too.

Penny Pincher: Zachary Taylor (1784–1850) almost lost the nomination for president when the letter asking him to accept the honor was returned unopened by Taylor because it had been sent "postage collect" and Taylor didn't want to pay for the postage.

Cheeky Advice: Abraham Lincoln grew his beard on the advice of 11-year-old Grace Bedell (shown below at age 14) of Westfield, New York, who had definite ideas about fashion. In a letter dated October 15, 1860, she wrote: "If you will let your whiskers grow . . . you would look a great deal better for your face is so thin. All the ladies like whiskers and they would tease their husbands to vote for you and then you would be President." Lincoln took Grace's advice, and, on his way to Washington in 1861, he stopped at the Westfield train station and thanked her in person for her suggestion.

House of a Different Color: The White House wasn't always white. It was originally gray and was referred to as the Presidential Mansion. It was painted white to cover the fire damage caused by Canadians fighting for the British forces during the War of 1812. From that time on, it was known as the White House.

One for the Books!

In addition to a swimming pool and a movie theater, the White House is equipped with its own . . .

a. bowling alley.
b. Starbucks café.
c. indoor miniature golf course.
d. petting zoo.

Showing His Metal: When Andrew Jackson (1767–1845) was running for president, his opponents had a lot of "ammunition" to use against him. He'd been in at least 14 fights, duels, and free-for-alls, and had three bullets still in his body to show for it!

No Frills:
George Washington
believe in getting
right to the point.
At just 135 words,
his second inaugural
speech is the
shortest in history.

The Long and the Short of It: President William Henry Harrison
(1773–1841) gave the longest inaugural address—8,443
words—and served the shortest term. He made his
nearly two-hour-long speech while standing outside on a
cold, snowy day, and caught a severe cold that turned
into pneumonia. Harrison died a mere 31 days after
taking the oath of office.

Short and Sweet: Abraham Lincoln felt he had failed miserably in writing the Gettysburg Address because he thought it was too short.

Making Headlines:

A heckler threw a cabbage at William Howard Taft (1857–1930) as he was making a speech. But, without missing a beat, Taft caught the cabbage, held it up so everyone could see it, and said, "I see that one of my adversaries has lost his head."

One for the Books!

No one has ever been elected president who was . . .

a. a divorced man.
b. a bachelor.
c. an inventor.
d. an only child.

Winning Words: Unlike most politicians, Calvin Coolidge (1872–1933) was shy and didn't especially like the sound of his own voice. At a dinner party one evening, a guest made a bet that she could get him to say more than two words. "You lose," Coolidge replied.

I Do's and Don'ts: In June 1886, Grover Cleveland (1837–1908) became the only president to get married in the White House. The bride, Frances Folsom, was 21 years old—27 years younger than Cleveland. In most weddings, the wife promised to obey her husband, but Cleveland requested that this be removed from the vows.

In the Pink: On a trip to Japan, William Howard Taft's wife, Helen, so charmed the mayor of Tokyo that he sent her 3,000 cherry trees. To this day, tourists flock to Washington, D.C., to see the cherry trees bloom in the spring.

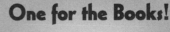

One for the Books!

Woodrow Wilson's second wife, Edith, was descended from . . .

a. Abigail Adams.
b. Clara Barton.
c. Pocahontas.
d. George Washington.

Make a Wish: Ulysses S. Grant's beloved only daughter, Nellie, was born on July 4, 1855—and for years, no one let on that the huge party complete with fireworks thrown every year on her birthday was not just for her.

Track Star: In the early 1860s, Abraham Lincoln's son Robert Todd Lincoln (1843–1926) was a student at Harvard University. While waiting to board a train at a crowded railroad station, Robert was pushed up against the train. When it started to move, he was knocked down and slipped, feet first, between the train and the edge of the platform. A quick-thinking man yanked Robert back onto the platform before he could be crushed.

Who was the man? Edwin Booth, an actor and brother of John Wilkes Booth—the man who would later assassinate Robert's father!

Tea for Two: When Abraham Lincoln was president, he kept two goats, Nanny and Nanko. He had harnesses made for them so that they could pull his son Tad in a little cart. One day, Mrs. Lincoln was entertaining in the East Room when Tad and the goats came galloping in, upsetting the tea cart and frightening the guests. That was the end of the tea party!

All in the Family: The six children of Teddy Roosevelt (1858–1919) did not have pets—they had a zoo! With dogs, cats, snakes, horses, rabbits, ducks, horned toads, a pig, a macaw, a badger, a pony, several guinea pigs, and a rat, visitors never knew what manner of creature they might find roaming the White House!

For the Birds:

Thomas Jefferson (1743–1826) loved mockingbirds—and kept several in the White House. His favorite, Dick, loved to sing along while Jefferson played his violin. Hopping up the stairs one at a time, Dick would follow Jefferson to his bedroom, where he perched nearby and sang the president to sleep.

Got Milk?

President William Howard Taft had a cow named Pauline Wayne that lived in the garage with his four automobiles. Pauline's milk was served each morning at the White House.

One for the Books!

Thomas Jefferson introduced many new foods to the U.S. that he'd discovered on his travels. Among them were macaroni, waffles, and . . .

a. cheese blintzes.
b. gyros.
c. burritos.
d. ice cream.

White House Bandit:

President Calvin Coolidge and his wife, Grace, had a pet raccoon named Rebecca. Rebecca was allowed to come inside to play—especially when there were visitors. Guests screeching at the "wild animal" in the White House never failed to make the president laugh.

Cold-blooded Gift:

After the Marquis de Lafayette (1757–1834) of France presented him with an alligator, President John Quincy Adams (1767–1848) kept it in the East Room of the White House.

One for the Books!

Franklin Roosevelt's dog, Fala, had a bald spot on his back because . . .

a. people snipped off his hair for souvenirs.
b. an infection made his hair fall out.
c. the secret service made him so nervous his hair fell out.
d. the president's grandchild learned to walk by holding on to his back.

Fala the Informer: A little black Scottie named Fala was the constant companion of Franklin Delano Roosevelt (1882–1945). During wartime, it was important to keep the president's travel plans a secret—which is why the men who guarded the president had a special name for the dog. They called him "The Informer," because a Fala-sighting meant that the president couldn't be very far away.

A Howlin' Good Time: President Lyndon B. Johnson (1908–1973) had two beagles he named Him and Her. He also had a stray mutt that he called Yuki. For laughs, he taught to Yuki to "sing" and, from time to time, he would join the dog in a howlingly good duet.

Don't Forget to Wash Your Hands! On July 2, 1881, an assassin shot President James Garfield as he walked through a Washington, D.C., train station. Garfield was taken to the White House, where Willard Bliss, the first of 16 doctors, tried to find the bullet without washing his hands or sterilizing the metal probe. Bliss didn't find the bullet and neither did the other doctors. Alexander Graham Bell looked for the bullet with an early metal detector that actually worked. But he couldn't find it either, because Garfield happened to be lying on a newly purchased mattress that had metal coils inside. On September 19, Garfield died from a heart attack probably brought on by infection. Where was the bullet? Harmlessly lodged in a muscle a few inches away from his spine. If the doctors of the time had understood the importance of sterilizing, Garfield might have made a full recovery.

Crowd Control: Immediately after President William McKinley (1843–1901) was fatally shot, he tried to keep an angry mob from attacking his assassin, saying, "Boys, don't let them hurt him!"

The Pits: On the hot July 4 of 1850, President Zachary Taylor attended groundbreaking ceremonies for the Washington Monument. He then went back to the White House, where he ate a bowl of cherries and drank a pitcher of ice-cold milk. Shortly afterward, he got severe indigestion. None of the doctors' treatments worked and, five days later, Taylor died. Rumors that he had been poisoned lasted for so long that in 1991 his body was exhumed and tested for arsenic poisoning. Nothing was found.

One for the Books!

John Adams and his friend Thomas Jefferson both died on . . .

a. Christmas Eve.
b. their birthday.
c. New Year's Day.
d. the Fourth of July.

Bull Shot! Theodore Roosevelt was shot in the right lung during his 1912 campaign for the presidency. Nevertheless, he made a scheduled campaign speech a few hours later, saying, "There is a bullet in my body, but it takes more than that to kill a bull moose."

One for the Books!

Harry S. Truman's middle initial stands for . . .

a. Sherman.
b. Stephen.
c. "S."
d. Sanders.

Brain Buster

America the beautiful. America the brave. But America the bizarre?!! Who would've guessed that three of these American facts are tried and true? Just one is totally false.

a. Sure, the words of "The Star-Spangled Banner" were written by Francis Scott Key—but it was not originally a song. It started out as a poem called "Defense of Fort McHenry."

Believe It!   **Not!**

b. Senator Strom Thurmond of South Carolina once delivered a speech to the senate that lasted 24 hours and 18 minutes.

Believe It!   **Not!**

c. The cable car, a symbol of San Francisco, California, is America's only official *moving* national historical landmark.

Believe It!   **Not!**

d. In honor of America's bicentennial in 1976, pastry chef Lynn Centrelli created the world's largest apple pie. More than 50 feet in diameter, the pie was made from more than 30,000 apples.

Believe It!   **Not!**

BONUS GAME—HISTORY MYSTERY

A number of men have all held the same job at different times throughout history. But before they took on this role, they were lawyers, teachers, governors, actors, farmers, and tailors. Eventually, they all ended up doing this same important job. What is it?

4 Been There, Done That!

It's interesting to see how quickly ideas that once seemed brilliant lose their luster as the years go by.

Looking Sharp:
Ancient Mayans frequently filed their teeth and used jewels to make them sparkle.

One for the Books!

In 1500 B.C.E., ancient Assyrians wore their hair . . .

a. in dreadlocks.
b. cut in the shape of tiered pyramids.
c. piled high in upsweeps.
d. in braids down to their waists.

All the Buzz: In ancient Greece, women wore live cicadas held on golden threads as ornaments for their hair.

Live Action:

The well-known game of Parcheesi was adapted from *pachisi,* a traditional game played in India since the 1500s. Most people played on cross-shaped "boards" made of cloth. But the Mogul Emperor Akbar had his own way of playing. He stood in the center of a huge board marked out in his courtyard and directed the movements of young slave women based on the roll of his dice.

One for the Books!

Flemish women in 15th-century Belgium wore such full, billowing skirts that they had to . . .

a. sit in tall chairs while dining.
b. have their doors widened.
c. change into dressing gowns to sit at the table.
d. wear weights to keep from being swept away on windy days.

Always in Style: The ancient Egyptians were so attached to their style of dress that they didn't change it for nearly 3,000 years!

No Yolk: Incan noblemen wore solid-gold ear ornaments that were as large as eggs.

Fashion Statement:

After the Reign of Terror ended in 1794, French women honored relatives who had been beheaded by wearing a red ribbon around their necks and cropping their hair short, like that of the victims.

Rags to Riches:

In the 1400s, the Duke of Burgundy invaded what is now Switzerland. He was defeated and fled, leaving his tents and all their furnishings behind. The impoverished Swiss soldiers tore everything apart and turned the material into patchwork uniforms slashed and puffed with different color fabrics. The costume was adopted and embellished by crack German soldiers called Landsknechte and, by the 16th century, the "slash-and-puff" style had become all the rage, worn by men and women all over Europe.

Party On!

Emperor Elagabalus (204–222) of Rome really liked to treat himself well. His daily dinner cost 300,000 sesterces—equal to $260,000 today. He also filled a pond with rose perfume and enjoyed boating on a reservoir filled with wine.

Galloping Grooms:

The six-horse sleigh used by the mother of Czar Peter the Great (1672–1725) of Russia was always accompanied by 12 grooms, one for each horse plus six others to try to help the sleigh move faster. All the grooms had to run steadily for miles.

Rich Diet: During the course of her adult life, Tz'u-hsi (1835–1908), empress of China, ate ten pounds of pearls. Over a period of 47 years, $2,000,000 worth of pearls were ground up in the imperial tea. Why? Because the empress thought they would guarantee her a youthful glow.

Big Cover-up: During the Victorian era (1838–1901), modesty was so important in Europe and North America that even furniture legs had to be covered up! Words relating to personal etiquette and hygiene could not be spelled out in print. When "petticoats" appeared in an article, it would be spelled "p-tt-c-ts."

One for the Books!

For 58 years, at a total cost of $2,813,000, Rani Bhanwani (1748–1806) of Nator, India, ordered that honey be poured into every ant hole to . . .

a. attract bears to devour the ants.
b. plug up the holes.
c. provide work for the unemployed.
d. ensure that no ant would ever go hungry.

Mr. Clean: The mystic Khan Jahan Ali of Khulna, India, was one of the most fastidious men in history. In the 15th century, he built 360 artificial lakes so he could bathe in a different one each day of the Muslim year.

Good Deal!

One day, when Countess Katarzyna Kossakowska (1716–1801) of Warsaw, Poland, forgot to bring her purse to the market, she paid for a basket of oranges by removing her string of rare oriental pearls and exchanging one pearl for each orange.

Wigged Out! After losing her hair at the age of 50, Countess Natalia Saltykoff (1737–1812) of Russia kept the fact that she wore a wig secret for 25 years by imprisoning a succession of hairdressers in an iron cage in her dressing room.

Breeches of Etiquette: In the 1750s, breeches were worn so tight in Alexandria, Virginia, that men had to climb onto a raised platform to step into them.

Hair Today, Gone Tomorrow:

Emperor Theophilus, who ruled the Eastern Roman Empire from 829 to 842, went completely bald in the year 840 and promptly ordered every man, woman, and child to shave his or her head. The penalty for not shaving was death!

One for the Books!

Prince Edward (1330–1376) of England was only 16 years old when he led the defeat of the French army at Crécy. He was called the Black Prince because he . . .

a. had long, black, curly hair.
b. was always dressed in black from head to toe.
c. wore black armor.
d. had all his rooms painted black.

All Stirred Up:

In Modena, Italy, a marble statue built in 1473 was a legal yardstick for the maximum length of women's dresses. Women who wore longer dresses could be punished for stirring up dust as their hems swept the ground.

Dressed to Impress:

Queen Elizabeth I of England had 2,000 gowns, all of which were kept in a separate clothing house.

Beauty Hurts!

Though cosmetics were very big during the 16th century, safety testing was not. So when women used products containing mercury to remove brown spots, warts, and other blemishes from their skin, they had no idea that it might also remove the outer skin layer, cause their teeth to fall out, and eventually cause severe mental illness!

One for the Books!

Women in 16th-century England wore their wedding rings on . . .

a. a chain around their neck.
b. their middle finger.
c. their pinky.
d. their thumb.

Fuzzy Thinking

Panta-loons! In 1933, the chief of police asked actress Marlene Dietrich to leave Paris, France, because she'd committed a shocking crime—wearing pants in public.

Half-baked: It may be hard to believe, but less than a century ago, it was illegal for half of the population (the female half) of the United States to vote!

NEW YORK STATE DENIES the VOTE To CRIMINALS LUNATICS, IDIOTS & WOMEN

Up in Smoke: Pablo Picasso, whose paintings now sell for millions of dollars, was once so poor that he burned his artwork to keep warm.

ALL THE

Fads come and go—and the more outrageous the better!

Stuff and Nonsense:
How many people can you stuff into a phone booth? In the 1950s, some people just had to find out.

Rock Hounds: In the mid-1970s, more than five million Pet Rocks were sold to people who wanted an easy-to-care-for pet that always behaved itself.

This box contains one genuine pedigreed.
PET ROCK

Crowning Glories:
During the 1700s, rich women loved to wear fanciful headdresses that were up to three feet tall and were covered with jewels, feathers, and other exotic decorations.

RAGE!

Sitting Pretty: Flagpole-sitting was a craze in the 1920s, and "Shipwreck" Kelly was the best. He once sat on a flagpole for 49 days straight!

Dance Fever: In the 1920s and '30s, "dance till you drop" was the motto of dance marathons. In 1930, one dance marathon in Texas lasted for 31 days, setting a world record.

SPY

Without Reservation: In the 1940s, the difficult Navajo language had not been written down, so it was used as a code for transmitting orders on the front lines during World War II. The code was never broken. In 2001, the Navajo "Code Talkers" were finally honored with Congressional Gold Medals.

Note-able Spy: In her day, singer Josephine Baker was as famous as Madonna. Maybe that's why no one suspected she was a spy for the French Resistance. Baker smuggled secret messages— which were written in invisible ink on her sheet music— throughout Europe.

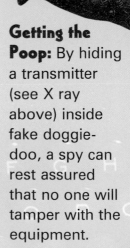

Getting the Poop: By hiding a transmitter (see X ray above) inside fake doggie-doo, a spy can rest assured that no one will tamper with the equipment.

GAMES

On the Line: Working as a servant in the Confederate White House, Mary Bowser spied on Jefferson Davis. She hung up the household's laundry according to a prearranged code to pass on military secrets to the Union.

Small Change: During the cold war of the 1950s, a paperboy discovered a hollow nickel among the change he collected. Inside was a tiny photograph of a coded message that was later connected to a Russian spy living in the United States.

Foolproof? With 150 quintillion possible settings, the Enigma machine turned out codes that the Germans were sure could never be broken. They didn't count on British mathematician Alan Turing, who cracked the codes, helping the Allies to win World War II.

White

Say Cheese! By the time George Washington was 57 years old, he had only one natural tooth left—but he did have six sets of dentures. They were made from the teeth of human cadavers, cows, elk, and even a rhinoceros. No wonder he rarely smiled!

The Real Skinny: President John Quincy Adams loved to skinny-dip in the Potomac River. One day, a reporter named Anne Royall sat on his clothes and refused to budge until he agreed to an interview.

Take That! The man who tried to assassinate Andrew Jackson was in for a surprise. After both the would-be assassin's shots misfired, the 72-year-old Jackson ran after him and beat him with his cane.

House Scoop

Top Dog: Warren G. Harding's dog, Laddie Boy, had his own valet and on his birthday, he got a cake made of dog biscuit layers held together with icing. Maybe his name should have been Lucky!

Shocking! Benjamin Harrison was the first president to have electricity in the White House, but it didn't do him much good. After he got a shock, he and his family were afraid to touch the light switches and often went to bed with all the lights blazing.

Tubmaster-in-Chief: At 300 pounds, William Howard Taft was so fat that he actually got stuck in the White House bathtub!

Stinky History

Did you ever wonder what people did before the flush toilet was invented?

Waste Not: In the Middle Ages, waste from the indoor toilets of rich people flowed down a shaft to a cesspool under the house. When the cesspool got full, it was emptied—and the "night soil" was used as fertilizer.

Going with the Flow: In ancient Rome, public toilets had stone seats set above flowing water. Much of the water was carried to the city in channels called aqueducts, which often flowed over rows of connected stone arches.

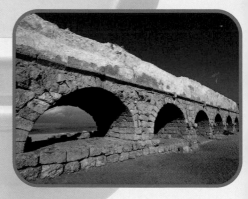

Party Poopers: In an ancient Greek lavatory, multiple seating made it possible to relieve oneself and socialize at the same time.

Brain Buster

Fashions come and go. But the most interesting ones tend to go down in history! Three of these humorous historical happenings are true. Can you guess which one is simply laughable?

a. The United States Mint considered making doughnut-shaped coins.

Believe It!   Not!

b. In 1939, Ernest Wright wrote a novel called *Gadsby*. It contained more than 50,000 words—but not one of them included the letter *e*.

Believe It!   Not!

c. In 1891, Silvain Dornon, a baker from Paris, walked up the 347 steps to the first platform of the Eiffel Tower—on stilts!

Believe It!   Not!

d. Hoffman and Klein Industries was an American manufacturer at the turn of the 20th century. In addition to basic stationery products, the company was also the first to manufacture the whoopee cushion, in 1902.

Believe It!   Not!

BONUS GAME—HISTORY MYSTERY

Throughout history, humankind has used a lot of energy. Vehicles, lights, stoves—we use energy in all kinds of ways. But in our entire history, we haven't used as much as this energy-guzzler does in just one second. What is it?

In order to trade goods and services, countries usually cooperate with each other. But every so often, a dispute that can't be settled may lead to war.

One for the Books!

In ancient Greece, soldiers lined their helmets and armor with . . .

a. mementos of loved ones.
b. sponges.
c. feathers.
d. burial instructions.

Timber! The Peace Poplar was planted in Jena, Germany, in 1815, to celebrate the end of the Napoleonic War with France. It suddenly toppled 99 years later on August 1, 1914—the start of World War I.

Before E-mail:

In 490 B.C.E., Persians invaded the Greek city of Marathon. Outnumbered, the Greeks sent their best runner, Philippides, to Sparta to ask for help. The Spartans refused, but the Greeks won the battle anyway. Elated, they sent Philippides, who had just

returned after running 200 miles in two days, to tell the folks back home in Athens. Eager to spread the news, Philippides made it to Athens, but had barely enough time to yell, "Nike!" (Greek for victory) before he dropped dead of exhaustion. In the photo, Robert Ripley is shown by the monument to Athenians who died in the battle.

Fine Feathered Steeds: In the

fifth century, the cavalrymen of Media, who won many battles against the Greeks, were mounted not on horses, but on ostriches.

Book Worm: Saheb Ibn Abad (C.E. 938–995), the scholarly grand vizier of Persia, always traveled with 117,000 books—even when he went to war. The library was carried on 400 camels that were trained to walk in line so that the library remained in alphabetical order and any book could be located quickly.

Heat of Battle: In 1402, the Battle of Ankara, Turkey, began by the Mongols stampeding a herd of 100 buffalo, each with a pot of liquid fire tied to its horns.

One for the Books!

In ancient times, Vikings settled disputes by binding themselves together at the waist and then . . .

a. stabbing each other.
b. seeing who could eat the most fish.
c. trying to knock each other out.
d. seeing who could sing the loudest.

Make Jokes, Not War:

The Battle of Buironfosse, in 1339, is usually thought of as one of the opening battles of the Hundred Years' War between France and England. In

fact, the battle never took place. Why? Because a frightened rabbit dashed back and forth between the lines of the two opposing armies. The sight was so hilarious that the soldiers on both sides roared with laughter and withdrew without exchanging a blow.

War Games: For
30 years, King Deva Raya (1424–1446) of Vijayanagar, India, ordered that arrows be shot toward three neighboring kingdoms each September. He then declared war on whichever country lay in the direction of the arrow that flew the farthest.

One for the Books!

Major Patrick Ferguson (1744–1780), leader of a corps of British sharpshooters, had a chance to shoot a famous American during the Revolutionary War, but he was too honorable to shoot a man in the back, and so spared the life of General . . .

a. Benedict Arnold.
b. Stonewall Jackson.
c. Israel Putnam.
d. George Washington.

Big Hold-up: In 1565, the Persian army attacked the city of Vijayanagar, India. Gulam Ali, an elephant belonging to the Persians, won the battle by winding its trunk around Rajah Ram, the enemy commander, lifting him up in the air, and holding him captive until his

troops surrendered. When the elephant died years later, an elaborate tomb was erected for it in the Indian city of Ahmandnagar.

Knight in Shining . . . Skirt? King Henry VIII (1491–1547) of England often wore a coat of armor with a pleated armor skirt. The skirt looked like cloth and was equipped with hinges so the monarch could ride horseback.

Tin Soldiers:

The hat issued to United States soldiers in 1870 was topped by a tin oil lamp that helped them find their way on dark nights.

Knight Lights:

When fighting battles after dark, knights in medieval times used lighted lanterns that were attached to their saddles.

Heady Escape: General Henry Heth (1825–1899) was leading Confederate soldiers in the Battle of Gettysburg when he was hit in the head by a Union bullet. Because his hat was two sizes too large, he had stuffed newspaper inside it to make it fit better. The paper deflected the bullet, and the general, though unconscious for 30 hours, recovered and lived another 36 years.

One for the Books!

In 1942, Lieutenant I. M. Chisov, a Russian soldier, lived to tell the tale after he . . .

a. was run over by a tank.
b. was shot by a firing squad for cowardice.
c. fell 21,980 feet from his fighter plane.
d. stepped on a land mine and was thrown 500 feet by the blast.

Hat Trick:
To make them look taller, Hessian soldiers (German mercenaries fighting for the British in the American Revolution) were issued hats that were 28 inches high.

Died in the Wool:
The assassination of Archduke Ferdinand of Austria was what triggered the start of World War I. But according to some historians, if the archduke had not been quite so vain, he might have survived. After Ferdinand was shot in Sarajevo on June 28, 1914, it was discovered that the buttons on his uniform were merely for show. The archduke had thought that the traditional button-down tunic was unbecoming, so he had asked the royal

tailor to create a pullover, form-fitting uniform that enhanced his profile instead. Had Ferdinand been wearing a real button-down tunic instead of one that had to be cut away, he might not have bled to death!

Psych! Legend has it that when a brash British officer challenged General Israel Putnam (1718–1790), famed hero of the American Revolution, to a duel, Putnam insisted that first they smoke their  pipes while sitting next to a powder keg with a burning fuse. After a few moments the Englishman fled in terror, only to learn later that the keg had been emptied of powder and refilled with onions.

One for the Books!

In the winter of 1861, some Union Army soldiers in Pennsylvania could not fire their guns because . . .

a. their mittens had no trigger fingers.
b. the triggers were frozen and wouldn't work.
c. they were too cold to fight.
d. they wanted to go home for the holidays.

Never Got a Break: George Washington was the only American soldier who served throughout the entire eight and a half years of the Revolution without a single leave of absence.

Weird but True: When the Civil War broke out, the leader of the Confederate forces, General Robert E. Lee (left; 1807–1870), and his family did not own slaves. However, Julia Dent, the wife of General Ulysses S. Grant, the leader of the Union forces, owned four slaves.

Perfect Pitch: In 18th-century France, the common people were poor and had nothing to eat. Angry and desperate, they revolted against the ruling class and defeated them. Afterward, they held trials, hauling the

rich before the French revolutionary tribunal. After her mother was condemned to death for being the wife of an enemy officer, Zoe de Bonchamps was ordered to sing for the tribunal's amusement. In a loud, clear voice, the little girl sang out, "Long live the King—down with the Revolution!" Her brave defiance so amused the judges that they released her mother at once.

Bird's-eye View: A Union soldier brought his pet eagle named Abe to keep him from getting too lonely during the Civil War. When the fighting started, old Abe would fly above the fray, then return to his master as soon it was over. Although the eagle did get shot, he survived his wounds and lived another fifteen years after the war. His remains are on display at the Wisconsin State Museum.

Time Out: Sometimes even soldiers need to take a break from war. One Confederate soldier wrote in his diary about the day that the sight of plump fresh blackberries prompted both sides to declare a truce. The soldiers picked the berries, shared some coffee, and traded newspapers . . . and then went back to fighting.

Hung Out to Dry: Elizabeth Van Lew was considered eccentric by many, but she was really a spy for the Union during the Civil War. On her recommendation, Mary Bowser, a slave Van Lew had freed years before, became a servant in the Confederate White House of President Jefferson Davis. Though Bowser played at being dimwitted, she was very intelligent and had a photographic memory. Perhaps if Davis had known that, he wouldn't have left military documents lying around. As it turned out, Bowser was one of the most valuable spies for the Union. She memorized military secrets she saw and overheard, then passed them back to Van Lew, who got them to General Ulysses S. Grant. Bowser also sent signals to Union soldiers in laundry code. For example, a white shirt hung beside an upside-down pair of pants meant "General Hill is moving his troops to the West."

One for the Books!

To protect them from sun and rain during the French Revolution, the National Guard of Paris was equipped with . . .

a. designer rain hats.
b. umbrella guns.
c. bulletproof raincoats.
d. portable mini-tents.

Close Shave: Captain James C. Whitley, a gunner in the Air Force during World War II, was recovering from his wounds in a hospital in Italy. One day, a barber who had been in the Italian air force was shaving him. During the conversation, Whitley discovered that the barber was a fighter pilot whose plane he had shot down in combat.

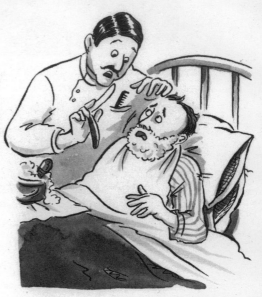

Grave Encounter: Brothers Grant and Karl Winegar, both marines stationed on Iwo Jima, Japan, had not seen each other for almost two years. Each fearing that the other might have been killed, they prowled through an American military cemetery, reading the grave markers—and suddenly met face-to-face.

One for the Books!

A sharpshooter who taught marksmanship during World War I was . . .

a. Belle Starr.
b. Mae West.
c. Annie Oakley.
d. Laura Ingalls Wilder.

Melts in Your Mouth: During World War II, soldiers needed quick-energy foods such as candy bars to keep up their strength. Other requirements were that the candy stay fresh in their backpacks and not melt in their hands. A sticky trigger finger could be a disaster! M&M's filled all these requirements and more. The fact that G.I.s bought M&M's when they came home made them an instant success with the general public.

Hail to the King: In 1360, King Edward III (1312–1377) of England was out to conquer France. But in April, just outside Paris, large hailstones rained down on his army, killing many soldiers and horses. Convinced that the hail was a sign from heaven, Edward signed the Treaty of Bretigny, giving up his claim to the French throne.

Birds of a Feather: A condor, the giant South American vulture, served as a customs agent with the Bolivian Customs Guard from 1941 to 1948 at a salary of $144 a month. The bird withdrew money every morning, flew to the meat market to buy veal for its daily meal, lived at the barracks with the rest of the company, and lined up for inspection twice a day.

One for the Books!

During World War II, money was smuggled into German prisoner of war camps in . . .

a. the linings of clothing sent by the Red Cross.
b. packets carried by homing pigeons that flew in at night.
c. packs of play money in Monopoly games.
d. rolls of gauze for bandages.

Brain Buster

Truly man's best friend, dogs have fought right alongside their masters in times of war. And they have been celebrated for their valiant work. Three of these canine heroes really exist. Can you spot the one that's doggone false?

a. A Labrador retriever named Bailey accompanied Paul Revere on his famous midnight ride. While Revere was yelling about the British, Bailey was barking out a warning to the other dogs in the towns, causing them to howl their owners out of bed.
Believe It!   Not!

b. A bull terrier named Stubby spent 18 months serving in World War I. As a member of the 102nd Infantry Regiment, Stubby located wounded soldiers, protected his regiment, and even caught a spy!
Believe It!   Not!

c. Max, a command dog in World War II, was able to obey orders from three different armies. He was trained by the Russians, then worked for the Germans, and eventually laid telephone lines for the British.
Believe It!   Not!

d. The United States Armed Forces K-9 Corps has trained "parachute dogs" to act as messengers, scouts, and guards. The dogs have parachuted in to do their jobs from heights of 1,500 feet and up!

Believe It!   **Not!**

• •

BONUS GAME—HISTORY MYSTERY

A certain heroic dog breed has been using its navigational skills, search-and-rescue techniques, and ability to withstand harsh environments for hundreds of years. The breed got its name because of its assistance to a certain group of monks. Archdeacon Bernard de Menthon founded a monastery in 1050 in the Swiss Alps on the border of Italy. The monks and their canine companions helped travelers navigate the treacherous pass between the two countries for centuries. Can you figure out the name of the dog breed?

POP QUIZ

History test! Don't worry, this isn't a *real* test. This is just a chance to prove how much you know about the bizarre and unusual—everything you've read about in this book! Weird and wacky history is totally unbelievable. But you already know that, right?

1. A 9,000-year-old piece of birch resin with teeth marks in it was evidence of ancient . . .
a. dental work.
b. chewing gum.
c. fake teeth.
d. cigarette smoking.

2. Which of the following languages is *not* on the Rosetta Stone?
a. Greek
b. Demotic
c. Egyptian hieroglyphics
d. Latin

3. Which of the following was discovered buried beneath the leaning tower of Pisa?
a. A house
b. A stable
c. A tomb
d. A time capsule

4. Evidence of the first taxicab in history was unearthed in New York City.

Believe It!   **Not!**

5. Which of the following historical love stories is true?
a. Theresa Cox, daughter of an Irish merchant, wed her true love in a secret ceremony, only to discover days later that she had married into the royal Dutch family.
b. The very afternoon that Sir Daniel Malino wed his bride, Princess Jillian of York, the nobleman was awarded a medal of honor for catching a thief who had been terrorizing the British countryside.
c. Nicolas and Claude François, the Duke and Duchess of Lorraine, escaped from prison together on April Fool's Day.
d. Italian spy Antonio Fiore was taken prisoner on a secret mission to Russia. His wife, Amie, dreamed of Antonio's capture the same night, and was able to accurately describe where her husband was being held.

6. Napoléon definitely had royalty in his blood. Which one of the following was *not* one of Napoléon's siblings?
a. Jérôme, king of Westphalia
b. Christopher Alloicious, duke of Jefferson
c. Louis, king of Holland
d. Elisa, grand duchess of Tuscany

7. In 1015 B.C.E., Heremon O'Neill won the land of Ireland in a . . .
a. polo match.
b. game of cards.
c. boating race.
d. lottery.

8. Honest Abe was honestly one of the most amazing presidents of the United States. Can you spot the one fact below that's *not* true?

a. During his presidency, Lincoln invented suspenders.

b. Lincoln's son was rescued from near death by the brother of the man who would assassinate his father.

c. Lincoln kept two goats named Nanny and Nanko.

d. Lincoln grew his beard on the advice of an 11-year-old girl.

9. President James Garfield could write with both his feet at once—with one foot he'd write in German, and with the other he'd write in Japanese.

Believe It!   Not!

10. Which of the following White House facts is false?

a. The White House was once gray.

b. The White House was once known as the Presidential Mansion.

c. The White House has housed a raccoon, a snake, a pig, and several mockingbirds.

d. The White House was originally supposed to be built in Vermont.

11. Which of the following fashion fads never even hit the runway, so to speak?

a. Greek women once wore live cicadas in their hair.

b. In Ancient Rome, children wore bow ties until the age of ten.

c. Ancient Mayans embedded jewels in their teeth.

d. Incan noblemen wore golden ear spools as big as eggs.

12. In a vain attempt to stay young-looking, Empress Tz'u-hsi of China ate ten pounds of what jewel?

a. Emeralds

b. Diamonds

c. Pearls

d. Opals

13. Queen Elizabeth I of England had so many of these items, she had to keep them stored in a separate house. What were they?

a. Thrones

b. Gowns

c. Shoes

d. Books

14. George Washington was the only American soldier in the Revolutionary War who did not take a leave of absence during the entire eight and a half years of fighting.

Believe It!   **Not!**

15. Because they don't melt in your hands, this candy was enjoyed by soldiers during World War II.

a. Snickers

b. Kit Kat

c. Peppermint Patties

d. M&M's

Answer Key

Chapter 1
Can You Dig It?
Page 5:   **c.** Keep out!

Page 6:   **b.** flowers.

Page 8:   **b.** create cartoons with speech balloons.

Page 10:   **b.** a seed from which flowers were subsequently grown.

Page 13:   **c.** mouse.

Page 15:   **b.** mud.

Page 16   **d.** eight seconds.

Brain Buster: b. is false.

History Mystery: The United States adopted daylight saving time.

Chapter 2
The Good Old Days?
Page 19:   **b.** sitting on the commode.

Page 20:   **c.** in fabric dyes.

Page 22:   **a.** night polo—using balls of fire.

Page 24:   **b.** king who lost a war.

Page 26:   **a.** death.

Page 28:   **d.** had taken only two baths in her life.

Brain Buster: c. is false.

History Mystery: Approximately 3¢ per acre

Chapter 3
Back in the U.S.A.
Page 31:   **a.** James Garfield.

Page 33:   **b.** lifting ships over shallow water.

Page 35:   **a.** bowling alley.

Page 37:   **d.** an only child.

Page 38:   **c.** Pocahontas.

Page 41:   **d.** ice cream.

Page 42:   **a.** people snipped off his hair for souvenirs.

Page 45:   **d.** the Fourth of July.

Page 46:   **c.** "S."

Brain Buster: **d.** is false.

History Mystery: President of the United States of America

Chapter 4
Been There, Done That!
Page 49:   **b.** cut in the shape of tiered pyramids.

Page 50:   **a.** sit in tall chairs while dining.

Page 53:   **d.** ensure that no ant would ever go hungry.

Page 55:   **c.** wore black armor.

Page 56:   **d.** their thumb.

Brain Buster: **d.** is false.

History Mystery: The sun

Chapter 5

Past Imperfect

Page 59:   **b.** sponges.

Page 61:   **a.** stabbing each other.

Page 62:   **d.** George Washington.

Page 64:   **c.** fell 21,980 feet from his fighter plane.

Page 66:   **a.** their mittens had no trigger fingers.

Page 69:   **b.** umbrella guns.

Page 70:   **c.** Annie Oakley.

Page 72:   **c.** packs of play money in Monopoly games.

Brain Buster: a. is false.

History Mystery: Saint Bernard

Pop Quiz

1.   **b.**
2.   **d.**
3.   **a.**
4.   **Not!**
5.   **c.**
6.   **b.**
7.   **c.**
8.   **a.**
9.   **Not!**
10.   **d.**
11.   **b.**
12.   **c.**
13.   **b.**
14.   **Believe It!**
15.   **d.**

What's Your Ripley's Rank?

Ripley's Scorecard

Nice work, history genius! You've dug up all kinds of fictions in these brain-busting activities. Now it's time to tally up your answers and get your Ripley's rating. Do you need to **Hit the Books**? Or maybe you already know that **The Past Is a Blast**! Add up your scores to find out!

Here's the scoring breakdown. Give yourself:
★ **10 points** for every **One for the Books!** you answered correctly;
★ **20 points** for every fiction you spotted in the Ripley's Brain Busters;
★ **10 points** every time you solved a **History Mystery**;
★ and **5 points** for every **Pop Quiz** question you got right.

Here's a tally sheet:
Number of **One for the Books!**
questions answered correctly: _____ x 10 = _____

Number of **Ripley's Brain Buster**
fictions spotted: _____ x 20 = _____

Number of **History Mystery**
puzzles solved: _____ x 10 = _____

Number of **Pop Quiz** questions
answered correctly: _____ x 5 = _____

Total the right column for your final score: _____

0–100
Hit the Books . . .

History is being made every day—and you don't want to miss it! The past is filled with funny, hard-to-believe stories. But maybe historical happenings just aren't your thing. No problem! There are other Ripley's books to explore. Is spooky and scary your bag? Try *Creepy Stuff*! Or *Bizarre Bugs,* if you're into the creepy crawly insect world!

101–250
Getting a Knack for Facts

The strange mysteries of history are starting to sound pretty cool, huh? You're developing a great eye for the unbelievable. And the world of Ripley's holds so many wacky and zany facts. Welcome! The bizarre is waiting around every corner.

251–400
The Past Is a Blast!

You know what fun history can be—especially when it's weird and wacky! And since history is bound to repeat itself, you're totally prepared for the future, too! To top it off, you can separate reality from the unreal in seconds—most of the time. Keep searching for the out of the ordinary. Just like Robert Ripley, you're bound to find it everywhere.

401–575
Time Traveler?

Do you have a time machine? Your knowledge of history is so good it's scary! Prehistory, the Middle Ages, modern times—nothing can stump you! Just like Robert Ripley himself, you know that there is cool stuff to be learned in every age. And you have a sharp eye for telling fact from fiction. Congratulations! You've got the makings of a fabulous historian!

Believe It!®

Photo Credits

Ripley Entertainment Inc. and the editors of this book wish to thank the following photographers, agents, and other individuals for permission to use and reprint the following photographs in this book. Any photographs included in this book that are not acknowledged below are property of the Ripley Archives. Great effort has been made to obtain permission from the owners of all materials included in this book. Any errors that may have been made are unintentional and will gladly be corrected in future printings if notice is sent to Ripley Entertainment Inc., 5728 Major Boulevard, Orlando, Florida 32819.

Black & White Photos

7 Trepanned Skulls (LC-USZC4-2536 LC-USZ62-115187); 20 Shakespeare (LC-USZ62-104495); 23 William Blackstone (LC-USZC4-2536); 26 Privy (HABS SC,10-CHAR,265B-1);
35 White House (LC-USZC4-405); 38 Grover Cleveland Wedding (LC-USZ62-5946); 42 Grace Coolidge and Raccoon (LC-USZ62-100816); 44 Garfield Assassination (LC-USZ62-7622); 46 Theodore Roosevelt (LC-USZ62-95887); 53 Tz'u-hsi (LC-USZ62-25833); 56 Queen Elizabeth I (LC-USZ62-120887); 67 Ulysses S. Grant; 67 Robert E. Lee/Library of Congress, Prints & Photographs Division

11 Rosetta Stone/© Copyright The British Museum

13 Golden Mummy/© Sandro Vannini/CORBIS

14 Hal Saflieni Hypogeum/© Paul Almasy/ CORBIS

16 Bust of Diocletian; 24 Mother Goose; 65 Archduke Ferdinand and Wife/© Bettman/ CORBIS

31 John Hanson/Cedric B. Egeli, c. 1974, oil on canvas. Courtesy Maryland Commission on Artistic Property, MSA SC 1545-1033

32 Courtroom; 36 Washington's Inauguration; 51 Landsknechte costume; 54 18th-century Breeches; 68 Eagle/Dover Publications

34 Grace Bedell/Copyright Unknown

39 Nellie Grant/Courtesy of Dr. James Brust, San Pedro, CA

43 Lyndon B. Johnson and Yuki/Yoichi R. Okamoto/LBJ Photo Library

71 M&M's/™/®M&M'S is a registered trademark of Mars, Incorporated and its affiliates (Mars, Incorporated 2002). Mars, Incorporated is not associated with Nancy Hall, Inc., Ripley's Believe It or Not!, or the authors. Images of Packaging printed with permission of Mars, Incorporated.

Color Insert

Marlene Dietrich/© Hulton-Deutsch Collection/ CORBIS

Suffragettes/Culver Pictures

Pablo Picasso; Phone Booth Stuffing; 18th-century Headdress; Flagpole Sitter/© Bettmann/CORBIS

Pet Rock/www.Super70s.com

Dance Marathon; Roman Aqueduct/© CORBIS

Navajo Code Talkers/Michael Kleinfeld/UPI

Josephine Baker (LC-USZ62-93000)/Library of Congress, Prints & Photographs Division, Carl Van Vechten Collection

Dog Doo Transmitter/Laura Miller

Confederate White House/Documenting the American South (http://docsouth.unc.edu), The University of North Carolina at Chapel Hill

FBI Nickels/Courtesy of the FBI

Enigma Machine/Zuma Press

Washington's Dentures/Courtesy of National Museum of Dentistry, Baltimore, MD

Women Voters (background); Andrew Jackson (LC-USZ62-5099); John Quincy Adams (LC-USZ62-7574); Warren G. Harding and Laddie (LC-USZ62-65041); Benjamin Harrison (LC-USZ61-480); William Howard Taft (LC-USZ62-7757); White House (background)/Library of Congress, Prints & Photographs Division

Middle Ages Privy/Weald and Downland Open Air Museum

Ancient Greek Lavatory/Penny Tweedie/Panos Pictures

Toilet (background)/PhotoDisc

Cover

Easter Island Moai/PhotoDisc

Washington's Dentures/Courtesy of National Museum of Dentistry, Baltimore, MD

Lyndon B. Johnson and Yuki/Yoichi R. Okamoto/LBJ Photo Library

Pet Rock/www.Super70s.com

If you enjoyed **Blasts from the Past**, get ready for

 **Awesome Animals!**

You'll be amazed at all the awesome things our furry and feathered friends can do. Read about . . .

Twelve elephants who play the instruments in an orchestra in Thailand

Rupert, the "Super Parrot" who once saved his owner from a burning house

Pigs who use their snouts to control the joysticks when they play video games for M&M's

Koko, a lowland gorilla who has a vocabulary of over 1,000 signs and understands 2,000 words of spoken English

These are just a few of the incredible stories you'll find in **Awesome Animals!** You might just discover that animals are a lot smarter, braver, and more unbelievable than you thought!